A Book of Mindfulness

Meditation
for Children

Shelley Wilson

illustrated by **Phaedra Elson**

bhc
press

Livonia, Michigan

Edited by Susan Cunningham

Meditation for Children
Copyright © 2019 Shelley Wilson
Artwork Copyright © 2019 Phaedra Elson

Published by BHC Press
Library of Congress Control Number:
2018930791

ISBN Numbers:
Hardcover: 978-1-64397-041-7
Softcover: 978-1-947727-40-3
Ebook: 978-1-948540-55-1

For information, write:
BHC Press
885 Penniman #5505
Plymouth, MI 48170

Visit the publisher at:
www.bhcpress.com

Table of Contents

For Olivia

Without your open mind and curiosity
this book would never have been born.

Introduction

Meditation has played a huge part in my life for many years, and I shared this with my own children when they were dealing with exam stress, friendship worries, and other anxieties that crop up day to day. My only regret is that I didn't meditate with them when they were much younger as I know it would have helped them through some of the tough times they've experienced.

My children are all approaching adulthood now, but they fully understand the importance of having a timeout, whether that's to be quiet, contemplative, or still, or to engage in being creative and productive. I hope that when they go on to have children of their own, they will remember the wonderful benefits they experienced and share meditation with their families.

* * * * *

The value of meditation has been written about many times, but this is predominantly targeted at adults. I wanted to share something that could be enjoyed as a family, or even as a classroom activity, which would benefit both adult and child.

Some people believe that meditation empties your mind. I've never found this to be possible. For me, meditation is the ability to notice my thoughts but not dwell on them.

I also use meditation to focus those thoughts on a single task. That activity could be a breathing exercise, a candle flame, counting, or something else, such as a guided visualisation (a story). We want our children to gain a sense of control over their thought patterns and their emotions so they can be more aware and understanding, and regular meditation helps with this.

Meditation calms an overactive mind and soothes an over-exerted body. It can boost creativity and reduce stress. As mentioned earlier, even very young children have worries and can experience stress or depression. In preschoolers, anxiety can be caused by separation from parents. Once older, academic and social pressures can cause our children to feel overwhelmed. Meditation is an accessible tool to support your child's positive mental health by developing and strengthening their ability to calm thoughts and actions.

Benefits Include:
- Improved memory
- Self-awareness
- Physical relaxation
- Enhanced creativity
- Inner peace and calm
- Better concentration

There is no need for special equipment. Five to ten minutes spent reading with your child is enough to get them into a healthy habit of disconnecting from hectic routines and enjoying a healthier lifestyle.

I'm sure you've experienced a few moments of memory loss, like forgetting where you left your car keys or if you turned the iron off. Children are no different. Meditation helps your child focus the mind on what they're doing in a specific moment, which in turn improves their learning skills.

When I was a child, my mum used to play a memory game at my birthday parties. She would put ten items on a tray and show it to all of us for a few minutes, then she'd cover it with a tea towel, and we had to try to remember what was on the tray and write it down. The one with the most correct items on their list won a prize. It was a fun game, but it was also a marvellous way to flex our memory muscles. Bruce Forsyth did something similar on the hit UK game show *The Generation Game*, where the winners would watch prizes pass by on a conveyor belt and would win everything they could recall in forty-five seconds.

Try playing the memory game with your child, as well as using this meditation book, and you'll soon see a difference in them. Ideally, you want your child to stop operating on autopilot and to become more aware of their surroundings.

With the amount of technology our children are faced with every day, it's no wonder they can be so distracted. We structure extracurricular activities and allow them unlimited screen time and then become irritated if they don't concentrate when we need them to. Our poor kids don't stand a chance! Meditation can help with this as it allows them full control over their creativity, concentration, and ability to learn.

Think about a moment when your child was fully absorbed in a film, or colouring in a picture, or building Lego. I remember with absolute clarity watching my eldest son drawing a picture with his brow furrowed and his tongue sticking out slightly. It was an adorable sight and one that showed me he was totally captivated by the activity. Instead of disturbing him to see what he was drawing or congratulating him on his efforts, I left him alone to enjoy the moment.

A story holds a similar magic spell and captures a child's interest to the same extent. The meditation stories within these pages are designed with this in mind.

* * * * *

In this beautifully illustrated book, I share ten visualisation meditations specifically written for young children aged five to nine years old. Although this book can be used as a bedtime companion, meditation is not restricted to an evening routine. These stories can be enjoyed and explored at any time of the day or night.

It's worth noting that as the adult reader, you don't need to have any meditation experience to enjoy sharing this book with your child or class. I've included a 'how-to' guide in the next section to help you put together a relaxing and memorable experience that will teach your child the skills and benefits of regular meditation.

* * * * *

As a daily meditator and meditation tutor, I see firsthand the benefits of regular practice, and I hope that you, the story-teller, enjoy using this book as much as your child enjoys listening to the stories and imagining the scenes.

How-to Guide for Parents, Guardians, and Teachers

Allow your child to decide for themselves if they enjoy the meditation sessions or would prefer to treat this as a simple picture book. If they're happy to listen to the story but don't enjoy taking part in the breathing exercises, then don't worry. You're not going to gain anything by trying to force meditation on anyone.

It's important to remember that your child trusts you, so if you act in a caring, happy, and relaxed manner while reading through this book, they will be more likely to mirror your actions and gain more from the experience.

Over time, your child may begin to accept the breathing exercises as a normal part of the process. Kids thrive when there is a structure and routine to their day. Meditation is a wonderful way to bond and see them become more focused, creative, and confident.

We all know how much children love stories, and how they enjoy acting out the characters and developing through repetition. You might find that your child has a favourite meditation story from the selection here, which is great. Let them explore everything they want to about that tale, over and over if necessary, as this helps to lengthen your child's attention span. You might even feel inspired to add a few extra lines or create alternative endings.

* * * * *

As already mentioned, these stories can be read at any time, day or night. However, young children respond well to a routine, so if you decide to make this part of a bedtime ritual, it may become a very special time of the day that your child looks forward to.

The room should be comfortable, not too hot or cold, and with as few distractions as possible. Make sure you are all relaxed. Get your child to close their eyes.

Young children are well-known for their reduced attention span, so I've written these meditations taking that into account. They are all short, and as you read through them, your child will soon let you know which ones they prefer.

Even though the stories are brief, the time to read them can be extended by speaking in a slow, calm, and quiet voice. If you require further guidance, I've shared one of the meditations on Facebook. The short video demonstrates how I deliver a child's meditation and is accompanied by beautiful illustrations from artist and illustrator, Phaedra Elson of Pipistrelle Art.

I've included pause points *(pause)* when you can stop reading for a few moments to let the visualisation deepen for your child. With their eyes closed as you read, they will be forming a picture in their mind of what you are telling them. This is the creative process taking shape. In each story, there is a point where you can pause for a little while longer (approximately ten to thirty seconds) to allow your child to explore that part of the story in their mind. They may tell you what they're seeing, or they may happily play out the visualisation in silence until you start speaking again. I've included the prompt for this in every story so you know when to stop: *(Pause for approximately ten to thirty seconds to allow your child's mind to create this image).*

The length of time you allow for the pause will depend on the age and restlessness of your child. You may find that over time you can increase the pause time from ten seconds up to thirty seconds.

At the end of every meditation, I've added two options for how you can end the session. Option one (if doing this as a bedtime routine) is to end with "goodnight, sleep tight." Option two (if doing this during the day or as a classroom activity) is to end with a drawing exercise to allow your child to draw, paint, and colour their unique interpretation of the story they just heard.

* * * * *

Drawing

Doing a drawing exercise is great if you're reading these meditations during the day. I would still recommend that your child close their eyes as you read the story to them. Have paper, pencils, pens, and crayons handy. Once you've finished the meditation, allow your child time to draw what they saw in their mind. Let them interpret the story in their own way.

Although each tale includes a beautiful illustration, you could hide the image and see how your child translates the words into pictures. This can be a valuable exercise for your child's development and expression.

* * * * *

Let's Get Started

To begin your meditation session, it can be relaxing to start with a simple breathing exercise.

Breathing Exercise

It might seem a little strange to be teaching your five-year-old how to breathe, but developing an inner calm is what meditation is all about. If you do this together, it makes the exercise more fun. It's something you can do in preparation for reading the meditation. Your child or class will come to see this as part of the routine.

In a slow, calm, and quiet voice read the following:

Take a deep breath in through your nose *(demonstrate—point to your nose if necessary)*. And breathe out through your mouth *(demonstrate)*. Now see if you can do it with me *(breathe in and out calmly together—do about five breaths and then stop)*. Now breathe normally.

The breathing exercise is best done with your eyes closed. Once you've shown them what to do, you might want to suggest they keep their eyes closed so they are ready for the story.

Your child should be fairly relaxed after your breathing exercise. Make sure they are still sitting upright or cross-legged, comfortable, and with their eyes closed, and read the chosen story to them in a soft voice. Most of all, enjoy this special time.

the
Meditations

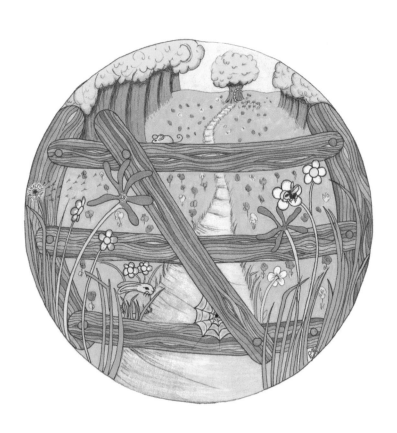

The Fairy Tree

Close your eyes and take a deep breath in through your nose and out through your mouth.

Now, imagine you are walking down a beautiful path surrounded by pretty flowers in every colour you can think of. There are pink flowers, yellow flowers, bright blue flowers, and ruby red roses.

Feel your arms and legs becoming more and more relaxed as you enter your special garden.

As you walk along the winding path, you see little animals scurrying through the undergrowth. Rabbits and squirrels chase each other under the bushes and in and out of the flowers. You can hear the bees flying lazily from flower to flower collecting the pollen.

You feel happy and safe in this special garden.

You come to an open space, which has a great old oak tree in the middle, but this is a special oak tree. It's a magic tree.

As you walk up to it, you see a pretty pink door in the side of the great old oak.

You turn the handle and step through.

Inside, you see lots of doors: fat ones, thin ones, wooden ones, and coloured ones. As you walk up a winding staircase, you see an oddly shaped door at the top of the stairs, and you open it. Inside, you meet a friendly fairy called Bella. She has bright yellow hair and a blue dress, and her wings are silver and flutter behind her.

You both decide to explore the great old oak tree together.

You can choose to look in any of the doors. Which one do you pick? What's inside? *(Pause.)*

Will you find the kitchen where the fairies are baking tiny cupcakes with pink frosting?

Will you find the sewing room where the fairies are mending their tunics and skirts?

Or will you find the great hall where the new fairies are learning to fly? *(Pause.)*

You turn the handle and open the door. You are in the great hall. As you watch the fairies, you feel your shoulders start to tingle, and when you look, you have a beautiful set of golden wings. You can flutter them and wiggle them and make them flap.

You and Bella join the other fairies and lift off the ground, flapping your new wings and spending some time flying around the great hall. You are laughing, whooshing through the air and swooping low, then soaring high. You are having so much fun. *(Pause for approximately ten to thirty seconds to allow your child's mind to create this image.)*

Your wings are starting to grow heavy. It's time to head home, so you wiggle your fingers and toes and stretch your arms. Your wings disappear, but they will be ready to use the next time you visit the great old oak. For now, you can dream about fairies and cupcakes with pink frosting, and maybe next time, you and Bella can visit the kitchen and do some baking. Until next time. *(Pause.)*

Option 1: Goodnight, sleep tight.

Option 2: Drawing—let's draw a picture of your adventure.

A Magic Carpet Ride

(approximately two minutes to read)

Close your eyes and take a deep breath in through your nose and out through your mouth.

It's early in the morning, and everyone is still asleep. You are snuggled up in bed when your bedroom window blows open and a magic carpet floats into your room.

You are happy and excited to see the carpet, and you jump out of bed and climb aboard the soft rug. Can you see what colour and shape it is? *(Pause.)*

The carpet shimmies and shakes as it waits for you to decide where you want to go on your adventure.

Today, you decide to visit the seaside. Your magic carpet is excited and flaps its tassels extra hard. It flies out of the bedroom window, getting higher and higher. You are so high in the sky, you can stretch up and reach the clouds. Your carpet rushes in and out of the fluffy white swirls, and the clouds tickle your nose.

The magic carpet dips and sways, and you break through the clouds and see the sparkling sea below you.

You both fly out over the water, dipping so low you can feel the spray of the sea on your face and see the fish in the water, and then you shoot up into the sky again to fly with the seagulls. The sun is shining, and the sea is calm. Are there any boats? What colours are their sails? How many clouds can you count? *(Pause for approximately ten to thirty seconds to allow your child's mind to create this image.)*

You are having so much fun, but your magic carpet is starting to get tired. It's time to head home, so you wiggle your fingers and toes and stretch your arms. Your carpet flies through your open window and back inside your bedroom, and you jump off, waving goodbye as you run and hop back into bed. The carpet shimmies and shakes before flying out of the window, but it won't be long until it visits again. For now, you can dream about the adventures you and your carpet can have on your next visit. Until next time. (*Pause.*)

Option 1: Goodnight, sleep tight.

Option 2: Drawing—let's draw a picture of your adventure.

Hello, Mr. Dragon

(approximately three and a half minutes to read)

Close your eyes and take a deep breath in through your nose and out through your mouth.

You are inside your house and begin walking toward the front door. Feel your arms and legs becoming more and more relaxed as you get closer and closer. You turn the handle and swing the door open wide.

Just outside your house is a large, scaly dragon. He has a big toothy smile, shiny scales, and huge feet. As you walk up to him, you can see all the other children on your street hiding behind the bushes. They are not as brave as you.

You feel happy and safe when you are with your dragon.

He lowers his large head so that you can climb onto his neck where you find a soft saddle with a seat belt strapped to his back. Once you are safely belted in, your dragon lifts his ginormous wings and flaps, flaps, flaps them hard.

He launches into the air, and you feel the wind ruffling your hair.

You are happy and safe on your dragon's back as you watch the ground get farther away.

The dragon swoops low to the road and then whooshes up high again. Your tummy flips and gurgles, and you laugh out loud.

As you circle over your house, the dragon shakes his mighty wings back and forth. He wants to know where you want to go and explore.

You choose to visit the park. Your dragon flaps his wings, and you take off, soaring over the rooftops of all the houses on your street. You can see the other children running along the pavement waving up at you.

In the distance, you can see the green grass of the park and the colourful swings and slides. Your dragon swoops down low, and you hear the excited cheers of the children playing. A lady is walking her dog and waves at you as you fly past.

The ducks on the great lake quack and squawk as you and your dragon zoom over the water and head out toward the football field. You spend some time circling the park, dipping so low you can hear the dogs bark, and then shooting up into the sky to fly with the pigeons. There are so many people at the park today. What can you see? How many dogs are there? What colour T-shirts are the footballers wearing? *(Pause for approximately ten to thirty seconds to allow your child's mind to create this image.)*

You are having so much fun, but your dragon's wings are starting to get heavy. It's time to head home, so you wiggle your fingers and toes and stretch your arms. Your dragon lands back outside your house, and you jump off his back, waving up at him as you run to your front door. He flaps his wings and smiles at you as he leaves, but it won't be long until he visits again. For now, you can dream about the adventures you and your dragon can have on your next visit. Until next time. (*Pause.*)

Option 1: Goodnight, sleep tight.

Option 2: Drawing—let's draw a picture of your adventure.

The Wizard's Spell Book

(approximately three and a half to read)

Close your eyes and take a deep breath in through your nose and out through your mouth.

It's raining outside, so you start looking for something to read. Then you find a huge book tucked at the back of the shelf. It's green, dusty, and really heavy. You open the front cover and find all the pages are blank.

You're about to put the book back on the shelf when you see swirly writing appear on the page. As you watch, you see two words emerge. 'Hello, [*insert your child's name*].'

This is a magic book, and you are so excited that it knows who you are.

The big book jumps onto the floor and does somersaults across the carpet. You chase after it and flip it open to another empty page. What will the book say next?

'I'm a wizard's spell book,' it writes. 'Shall we have some fun?'

You nod your head and clap your hands. It's fun to have a friendly magic book to play with.

The pages flip backward and forward until they fall open at a picture of a large, white feather.

The book writes a message in curly letters. 'Let's make this feather dance.'

The magic book lifts off the floor and starts to sway from side to side. You lift your arms and do the same thing, swaying your hands from one side to the other.

As you watch, the huge white feather floats off the page and out of the book. You move your hand to the right, and the feather follows. You move your hand to the left, and the feather follows. You can have lots of fun making the feather dance. What do you do next? Can you make it spin around? Can you make it float up to the ceiling? Does the feather change colour if you clap your hands? *(Pause for approximately ten to thirty seconds to allow your child's mind to create this image.)*

You are having so much fun, but your wizard's spell book is getting tired. It's time to put the book back on the shelf, so you wiggle your fingers and toes and stretch your arms. You slide the heavy book back on the shelf, and it snuggles down and starts snoring. You tiptoe away and let it sleep, but it won't be long until you can play together again. For now, you can dream about the fun you'll both have flipping through the pages to find another wizard's spell when the book wakes up. Until next time. (*Pause.*)

Option 1: Goodnight, sleep tight.

Option 2: Drawing—let's draw a picture of your adventure.

Teddy Bears' Picnic

(approximately two and a half minutes to read)

Close your eyes and take a deep breath in through your nose and out through your mouth.

Now, imagine you are skipping through the long grass on a sunny day. You are happy and safe and enjoying your time outside. You come across a large field with brightly coloured picnic blankets dotted all over the grass. Can you see the different colours and patterns? *(Pause.)*

You hear music drifting from the trees, and as you watch, you see a row of teddy bears walking toward you. They are laughing and singing and carrying big baskets full of treats.

They are really happy to see you and ask if you would like to join their picnic. You clap your hands and agree to stay for a while.

The teddy bears are all shapes, sizes, and colours. Some are small and fluffy, others are tall and skinny. Some have patches on their tummy, and others have multicoloured feet. Which one is your favourite? *(Pause.)*

They open up the picnic baskets, and you see all your favourite sandwiches, snacks, and treats. There's colourful fruit, carrot sticks and grapes, crisps and muffins, ham and cheese, and big bottles of water and juice. You and your teddy bear friends enjoy a wonderful feast. *(Pause.)*

Once you've finished your food, the teddy bears ask you to play some games, but they can't decide which one to play first. What's your favourite game? Is it hide-and-seek? Or maybe you like making daisy chains. How about musical statues?

You choose your favourite game and have fun playing with the teddy bears for a while. *(Pause for approximately ten to thirty seconds to allow your child's mind to create this image.)*

You are having so much fun, but the teddy bears are getting tired. It's time for them to go home, so you wiggle your fingers and toes and stretch your arms. They wave at you and then disappear into the trees. For now, you can dream about the fun games you'll play at the teddy bears' next picnic. Until next time. (*Pause.*)

Option 1: Goodnight, sleep tight.

Option 2: Drawing—let's draw a picture of your adventure.

Helicopter Fun

Close your eyes and take a deep breath in through your nose and out through your mouth.

Imagine you are walking through the park toward a big green field. Feel your arms and legs becoming more and more relaxed as you get closer and closer.

As you walk along, you can hear the *whirr* of a helicopter in the sky above your head. You look up and see it hovering over the grass. What colour is the helicopter? Can you see the pilot?

There are lots of children watching the helicopter as it lands, but some of them are holding their hands against their ears because the helicopter is so noisy. You don't mind the noise because you love the *pft pft pft* sound it makes.

The helicopter pilot sees you and waves. You smile and wave back.

He turns the engine off, and the big rotors start to slow down. The pilot opens up the door to the helicopter and shouts your name.

'[*insert child's name*], would you like to take a trip in the helicopter?'

You are so excited that the pilot picked you to go on a trip, and you rush to climb into the back seat. Once you are safely belted in, the pilot starts the engine, and the helicopter lifts off and rises higher and higher into the sky.

You are happy and safe in the helicopter as you watch the ground get farther away.

The pilot flies low over the heads of all the other children, and they run and wave at you as you whoosh past. You laugh out loud. They are running, but they can't keep up with the speed of the helicopter.

As you circle over the park, the pilot asks you where you want to go and explore.

You choose to visit the street where you live. The helicopter soars over the park and the roads. You can see the shops and your school and lots of people walking along the pavement waving up at you.

As you fly over the houses, you can see swings and slides in people's back gardens. A lady is hanging her washing on the line. Two fluffy white dogs dart around their garden, barking up at the sky as you fly past.

The pilot points down at the ground, and you can see your house and all your neighbours and friends playing out in the street. They cheer when they see you in the helicopter. You spend some time circling the street, dipping so low you can hear your friends laughing, and then rise up into the sky to hover over the roof of your house. It looks very different from above. What can you see from up here? Can you see your garden? What colour is the roof of your house? *(Pause for approximately ten to thirty seconds to allow your child's mind to create this image.)*

You are having so much fun, but the pilot is starting to get tired. It's time to head home, so you wiggle your fingers and toes and stretch your arms. The helicopter lands back in the big green field, and you jump out, waving up at the pilot. He smiles at you as he leaves, but it won't be long until he brings the helicopter back to visit again. For now, you can dream about the adventures you will take in the helicopter on your next visit. Until next time. *(Pause.)*

Option 1: Goodnight, sleep tight.

Option 2: Drawing—let's draw a picture of your adventure.

Dancing Shoes

Close your eyes and take a deep breath in through your nose and out through your mouth.

Now, imagine you are walking down a long path toward a pretty white building with big windows. Outside the doors are bright flowers in every colour you can think of. The path leads you to your very own dance school.

Feel your arms and legs becoming more and more relaxed as you get closer to the big doors and walk inside the hall.

You see lots of other girls and boys busy putting on their dance shoes. Everyone is excited to be there. Some of the children are wearing ballet shoes, some are wearing tap shoes, and others have sparkly black pumps. Which dance shoes do you want to wear today? *(Pause.)*

You feel happy and safe in your dance school.

There is plenty of space in the hall for everyone to have fun. Music starts to play, and all the boys and girls move into the middle and tap their feet.

You swing your arms from side to side and tap your foot on the floor. The music gets faster, and you begin to whirl around in circles with your arms stretched out. It makes you giggle as you spin around and around.

Suddenly, your dance shoes start to move on their own, taking you with them. They leap in the air and land gracefully back on the floor. They twirl and prance and tap and hop.

You can see all your dancing friends are doing the same. Their dance shoes are moving on their own too. Everyone is whirling and spinning and tapping and jumping.

You are laughing so much, whooshing around the hall, dancing, and twirling. You are having so much fun. What are your dance shoes doing now? Can you feel them tapping and jumping? Do they have a favourite dance? *(Pause for approximately ten to thirty seconds to allow your child's mind to create this image.)*

Your feet are starting to grow heavy, and your dance shoes are beginning to slow down. The music stops, and you know it's time to head home, so you wiggle your fingers and toes and stretch your arms. You take your dance shoes off, but they will be ready to use the next time you visit the dance school. For now, you can dream about ballet and tap dancing, and maybe next time, you can try a different kind of dance. Until next time. (*Pause.*)

Option 1: Goodnight, sleep tight.

Option 2: Drawing—let's draw a picture of your adventure.

Meet the Astronaut

(approximately three and a half minutes to read)

Close your eyes and take a deep breath in through your nose and out through your mouth.

Now, imagine you are walking through a large green field. Grass and buttercups cover the ground as far as you can see. Feel your arms and legs becoming more and more relaxed as you walk farther and farther. You reach a small hill and climb to the top.

From here, you can see lots of people, houses, and roads. As you look down from the hill, you see a shiny silver rocket with an astronaut standing by the big round door. He has a wide smile, a bright white suit, and he's carrying a helmet tucked under his arm.

He waves over to you to join him, and you run down the hill toward him. You can see other children watching the astronaut, and you feel proud that he picked you.

He wants you to join him on his adventures to see the stars, and you happily climb inside the rocket. There's a padded red seat for you to sit in with a seat belt and an astronaut's helmet of your own. You slip it onto your head and look at all the coloured buttons inside the rocket through the little window in your helmet.

You feel happy and safe inside the shiny silver rocket.

Once you are safely belted in, the astronaut flips a switch, and the engines start to shake as they get ready to launch you both into the sky. Ten, nine, eight, seven, six, five, four, three, two, one, lift off!

You launch into the air, and through your helmet, you can see outside the window and the children waving as you get higher and higher.

The rocket soars into the blue sky, and your tummy flips and gurgles. You laugh out loud.

As you look outside the window, the blue sky changes and becomes dark as you leave Earth. There are a million shining stars surrounding you. The astronaut flips a switch, and the rocket slows down and begins to glide through space.

You unbuckle your seat belt and begin to float in midair. The astronaut shows you how to do somersaults and to twist and spin without any gravity.

You are having so much fun.

Through the window, you can see the moon in the distance glowing bright. The astronaut turns the rocket, and you set a course for the moon.

There are so many stars in the sky as you travel closer and closer. Can you count them? *(Pause.)*

The astronaut flies the rocket closer to the moon, and you peek out of the window. What can you see? How many craters are there? Can you see the man in the moon? Are there any other spaceships in the sky? *(Pause for approxi-*

mately ten to thiry seconds to allow your child's mind to create this image.)

You are having so much fun, but the astronaut is getting tired. It's time to head home, so you wiggle your fingers and toes and stretch your arms. The shiny silver rocket lands back in the field at the bottom of the hill, and you jump out of the round door, waving back at the astronaut. He waves and smiles at you as he leaves, but it won't be long until he visits again. For now, you can dream about the planets you and the astronaut can see on your next visit. Until next time. (*Pause.*)

Option 1: Goodnight, sleep tight.

Option 2: Drawing—let's draw a picture of your adventure.

Let's Fly a Kite

(approximately two and a half minutes to read)

Close your eyes and take a deep breath in through your nose and out through your mouth.

Now, imagine you are wrapped up in a warm coat, hat, and gloves. It's a sunny day but very cold and windy. You are happy and enjoying your time outside. You love a windy day because it means you can fly your kite.

You are standing in a large field with lots of other children and their kites. Can you see the different colours and patterns? *(Pause.)*

You hold the kite string tightly in one hand and run along the grass as fast as you can before launching your kite into the sky. The wind takes it higher and higher, and you grip the string so it doesn't fly away. You can control how far your kite goes.

The wind blows, and your kite dips to the side and then circles back again. There are three long ribbons fluttering from the end of your kite, and you can see them twirling. What colour are they? *(Pause.)*

The kites in the sky are all shapes and sizes and colours. There are small red ones, large blue ones, butterfly-shaped ones, and multicoloured ones. Which one is your favourite? *(Pause.)*

The wind gets stronger, and as you hold the long string, you feel the tug of your kite high up in the sky. You are in control and can make your kite go in any direction you choose. Will you pull the string to the right and watch the kite dance, or will you pull the string to the left and watch your kite swoop? *(Pause.)*

What can you make your kite do? Is it the highest kite in the sky, or is there another one that's higher? Can you make it dance? How many other kites can you see? *(Pause for approximately ten to thirty seconds to allow your child's mind to create this image.)*

You are having so much fun, but your arms are getting tired. You pull on the string and wind your kite lower and lower until you can hold it in your hand. It's time to go home and have a hot chocolate, so you wiggle your fingers and toes and stretch your arms. For now, you can dream about the fun you'll have on the next windy day. Until next time. (*Pause.*)

Option 1: Goodnight, sleep tight.

Option 2: Drawing—let's draw a picture of your adventure.

The Sailboat

Close your eyes and take a deep breath in through your nose and out through your mouth.

Now, imagine you are walking along a sandy beach with lots of people making sandcastles and eating ice cream. Feel your arms and legs becoming more and more relaxed as you walk along the sand.

In the distance, you can see twenty sailboats bobbing up and down on the water. There are boats in every colour you can think of. There are white boats, yellow boats, bright blue boats, and red boats.

As you walk along the sand, you see families having picnics and eating sandwiches. There are small dogs and big dogs chasing each other and jumping in and out of the water. You can hear the seagulls squawking in the sky above.

You feel happy and safe at the seaside.

You walk into the water until you reach your sailboat. What colour is it? Does it have a bright sail? *(Pause.)*

You lift the anchor and pull on the rope that holds the sail in place. It flaps in the breeze, and you tie it in place. As the wind blows, you feel your sailboat start to move.

The water whips up around you, and you feel the spray of the sea on your face. The sun shines down on you, and you feel warm and happy. Your sailboat is moving across the water, and you wave at the children playing on the beach as you pass by.

You can choose where you want to sail. Where do you want to go? Do you want to visit the nearest island? Or do you want to sail to the next beach for ice cream?

Will you race with the other sailboats and see who is the fastest?

Will you collect shells on the beach and use them to decorate your boat?

Or will you try to spot as many fish in the sea as you can? *(Pause.)*

You pull on the ropes and adjust the sails. You are starting to catch up with the other sailboats. The wind pushes you along, and you wave at the other sailors.

You are laughing, whooshing through the water. You are having so much fun. How many sailboats can you see? What colour sails do they have? Can you spot any fish in the water? Is your sailboat the fastest? *(Pause for approximately ten to thirty seconds to allow your child's mind to create this image.)*

You are starting to get tired, so you turn your sailboat and head for home. You wiggle your fingers and toes and stretch your arms. Your sailboat will be ready to use the next time you visit the seaside. For now, you can dream about the adventures you'll have next time you go out in your sailboat. Until next time. *(Pause.)*

Option 1: Goodnight, sleep tight.

Option 2: Drawing—let's draw a picture of your adventure.

Creating Your Own Meditations

It's so easy to adapt any of these meditations and include adventures of your own. Let's take "The Fairy Tree" as an example. Within the guided visualisation, you are given three options: to bake in the kitchen, visit the sewing room, or explore the great hall. In our story, we learn to fly in the great hall. However, you could create a unique adventure for your child and choose one of the other options.

Follow the same pattern by keeping it short, speaking slowly and calmly, and giving your child plenty of time and space to interpret the story in their mind.

If you are using this as a classroom exercise, then perhaps your students could create an alternative adventure or ending.

Have fun and explore opportunities to invent mini-meditations that are special and distinct to you and your family.

Acknowledgements

The concept of *Meditation for Children* came about thanks to five-year-old Olivia. She wanted me to write her a personal meditation as she desperately wanted to come along with her mum to our meditation classes but it clashed with her bedtime! Thank you, Liv.

Thank you to my three children and parents for their unwavering support of everything I produce.

A huge thank you to the team at BHC Press and thanks to my wonderful editor, Sooz, for her continued guidance and friendship.

I'd also like to thank the hugely talented Phaedra from Pipistrelle Art who created the artwork illustrations.

About the Author

Shelley Wilson is an author and award-winning blogger, a meditation tutor, and qualified holistic health practitioner. She divides her writing projects between motivational non-fiction for adults and her young adult/teen fiction.

Her non-fiction books combine lifestyle, motivation, and self-help with a healthy dose of humour, and her YA novels combine myth, legend, and fairy tales.

Shelley was born in Leeds, West Yorkshire but raised in Solihull, West Midlands, UK, where she lives with her three children and a black cat called Luna. When she's not focused on her writing you will find her spending time with her family, running, or cooking up a gluten-free meal.

Visit Shelley at her author's website or her publisher's website:

www.shelleywilsonauthor.co.uk
and www.bhcpress.com

Lightning Source UK Ltd.
Milton Keynes UK
UKHW052210200622
404692UK00006BA/108